# The Gingerbread Man

Key sound ay spellings: a, ai, ay, ey
Secondary sounds: ea, er, ite

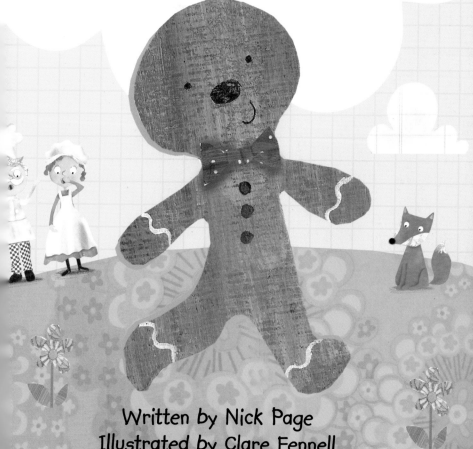

Written by Nick Page
Illustrated by Clare Fennell

# Reading with phonics

## How to use this book

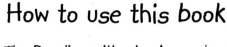

The **Reading with phonics** series helps you to have fun with your child and to support their learning of phonics and reading. It is aimed at children who have learned the letter sounds and are building confidence in their reading.

Each title in the series focuses on a different key sound. The entertaining retelling of the story repeats this sound frequently, and the different spellings for the sound are highlighted in red type. The first activity at the back of the book provides practice in reading and using words that contain this sound. The key sound for **The Gingerbread Man** is ay.

Start by reading the story to your child, asking them to join in with the refrain in bold. Next, encourage them to read the story with you. Give them a hand to decode tricky words.

Now look at the activity pages at the back of the book. These are intended for you and your child to enjoy together. Most are not activities to complete in pencil or pen, but by reading and talking or pointing.

The **Key sound** pages focus on one sound, and on the various different groups of letters that produce that sound. Encourage your child to read the different letter groups and complete the activity, so they become more aware of the variety of spellings there are for the same sound.

The **Letters together** pages look at three pairs or groups of letters and at the sounds they make as they work together. Help your child to read the words and trace the route on the word maps.

**Rhyme** is used a lot in these retellings. Whatever stage your child has reached in their learning of phonics, it is always good practice for them to listen carefully for sounds and find words that rhyme. The pages on **Rhyming words** take six words from the story and ask children to read and find other words that rhyme with them.

The **Key words** pages focus on a number of key words that occur regularly but can nonetheless be challenging. Many of these words are not sounded out following the rules of phonics and the easiest thing is for children to learn them by sight, so that they do not worry about decoding them. These pages encourage children to retell the story, practising key words as they do so.

The **Picture dictionary** page asks children to focus closely on nine words from the story. Encourage children to look carefully at each word, cover t with their hand, write it on a separate piece of paper, and finally, check it!

Do not complete all the activities at once – doing one each time you read will ensure that your child continues to enjoy the stories and the time you are spending together. **Have fun!**

There once was a crazy, old baker
and a crazy, old baker's wife,
and one day they made a gingerbread man,
who amazingly came to life!

The name that they gave him
was Gingerbread Fred
and they said, "Don't you wander away!
You are not a real boy, you're a pastry,
like the ones they serve in the café!"

But before you could say,

"CAKES AND BAGELS!",

Fred wouldn't obey – he ran off to play!

And Gingerbread Fred said . . .

"Run, run, run, as fast as you can,
you can't catch me,
I'm the gingerbread man!"

He made his way into a playground,
where a cat lay asleep by the gate.
"Oh, meow," said the cat.
"Here comes breakfast,
I wondered how long I should wait."

Meow!

But before you could say,
"CAKES AND BAGELS!",
Fred didn't delay,
but went on his way!

And Gingerbread Fred said . . .

"Run, run, run, as fast as you can,
you can't catch me,
I'm the gingerbread man!"

Next, Gingerbread Fred reached a farmyard, where a dog lay asleep in the hay.
"Oh, BOW-WOW!" said the dog.
"Must be lunchtime!
It's a gingerbread-cake takeaway!

Bow-wow!

But before you could say,
"CAKES AND BAGELS!",
Fred wouldn't remain,
but raced down the lane!

And Gingerbread Fred said . . .

"Run, run, run, as fast as you can,
you can't catch me,
I'm the gingerbread man!"

Then Gingerbread Fred reached the lakeside,

"Good day," said a fox by the bay.

"Need my aid?" said the fox. "I can take you.

You can ride on my back, just one way."

And before you could say,

**"CAKES AND BAGELS!"**,

Fred was persuaded, and in the fox waded.

And Gingerbread Fred said . . .

"Run, run, run, as fast as you can,
you can't catch me,
I'm the gingerbread man!"

The fox said, "May I make a suggestion?",
as they made their way over the bay.
"If you stay on my nose, you'll be drier,
and avoid all this splashing and spray."

Good day!

Quite soon, they were over the water, and Fred said, "Good day! Thanks again!"

"Not so fast," said the fox, "I've a brainwave, would you like to fly, just like a plane?"

And before you could say,

"CAKES AND BAGELS!",

with a cry of "wa-hey!",
Fred flew away!

And Gingerbread Fred said . . .

"Run, run, run, as fast as you can,
you can't catch me, I'm the . . ."

CRUNCH! SCRUNCH! MUNCH!
Fox ate him for lunch.

And Gingerbread Fred said . . .

Nothing. (Ever again.)

CRUNCH!
SCRUNCH!
MUNCH!

# Key sound

There are several different groups of letters that make the **ay** sound. Practise them by helping Gingerbread Fred make some sentences. Use each word in the bagels in a different sentence.

they
convey
obey
survey
prey

baker
made
ate lake
came
persuade
race lane
gave
plane
cake
made
make
wave
make
gate
bagel
take

remain
rain
main
train
wait
plain
paid
did
brain

say
play
stay
day
lay
spray
delay
bay
playground
hay
replay
away

25

# Letters together

Look at these groups of letters and say the sounds they make.

**ea**    **er**    **ite**

Follow the words that contain *ea* to help the baker find his bread.

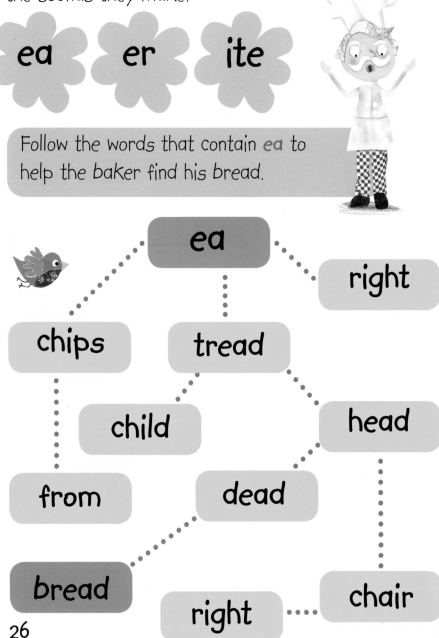

ea

right

chips    tread

child    head

from    dead

bread    right    chair

Follow the words that contain **er** to help the fox cross the river.

lots

er

other

later

dinner

water

fern

planner

cake

river

runner

Follow the words that contain **ite** to help the fox bite the biscuit.

suddenly

mite

ite

kite

white

site

quite

write

bite

# Rhyming words

Read the words in the flowers and point to other words that rhyme with them.

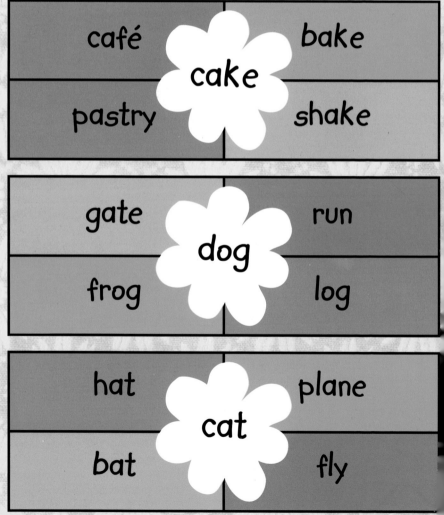

café     **cake**     bake

pastry     shake

gate     **dog**     run

frog     log

hat     **cat**     plane

bat     fly

life

knife

**wife**

lunch

back

main

baker

**brain**

bay

grain

lakeside

rose

**nose**

hose

flew

Now choose a word and make up a rhyming chant!

The baker **bakes cakes** and **makes milkshakes**.

29

# Key words

Many common words can be tricky to sound out. Practise them by reading these sentences about the story. Now make more sentences using other key words from around the border.

The fox ate Fred **for** lunch.

The baker said to Fred, "**Don't** you wander away!"

The cat and dog **couldn't** catch Fred.

The baker **made** a gingerbread man.

The **cat** chased Gingerbread Fred.

The gingerbread man **ran** from the baker.

something • animals • looked • got • it

• couldn't • town • a • sat • run • made • are • ran • w

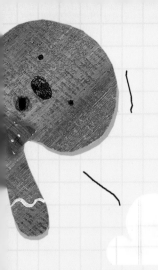

Fred said, "**Run, run, run,** as fast as you can!"

The fox swam across the **river**.

There once was a crazy, **old** baker.

The **dog** chased Gingerbread Fred.

for • cat • dog • river • don't • let • wanted • after • am • suddenly • up • you • make •

old • there • were • still • old • can't • took • think

# Picture dictionary

Look carefully at the pictures and the words.
Now cover the words, one at a time.
Can you remember how to write them?

bagel

baker

cakes

fox

lakeside

lane

playground

water

wife